A journal of humor and
political observation during
challenging times

To Lisetta,
  molto grazie!
I wish I had been
a better student for
you! you are a delight!
A rividerci!
        Ciao Bella

The COVID Collection of Pandemic Poetry

A journal of humor and political observation during challenging times

ISBN: 978-1-916852-50-1

Book Design: Queener Design
Copy Editor: Priscilla Donegan

Dedication

THIS BOOK IS DEDICATED TO MY DEAR HUSBAND, CHUCK QUEENER, WHO HAS been, and continues to be, my daily inspiration. His endless patience, creativity and cheerleading never cease to amaze me. He brings me unending joy.

I also dedicate this to our children and their spouses, who, like us, are living in challenging times, yet continue to move forward with hope and wisdom as they raise and nurture our wonderful grandchildren.

Our grandchildren are, perhaps, my greatest motivation for wanting this country to value truth. It is our responsibility as their elders to protect the present so that their futures will be safe and the planet habitable.

I hope that everyone I know and love will see calmer times, the preservation of democracy and will experience peace, joy, good health, and happiness.

Preface

SHORTLY AFTER WE BEGAN TO HUNKER DOWN FOR THE COVID-19 PANDEMIC IN 2020, I became particularly excited on April 20, when the mailman delivered several items we had ordered from Amazon — face masks, hand sanitizer, and silicone gloves. I became so giddy that I exclaimed to Chuck, my husband, "We'll start a little COVID Corner," and sat down to write a poem about that concept. A few days later I received an email blast from one of my high school friends, Harry, who wrote to our entire class that, 1) he hoped everyone would stay well and 2) he had been washing his hands so arduously that he discovered the answers to the 8th grade social studies test (about seven decades later)!

So many of our classmates responded with similar stay-well wishes and humorous comments that I was inspired to circulate my COVID Corner poem as well. I received unexpected responses urging me on, and so every Thursday I emailed the newest poem that had come into my head to hundreds of classmates, with continued notes back from people I hadn't connected with in decades. Many told me that I was expressing their thoughts exactly. Then I decided to add friends and family to my email list and received great encouragement to keep going. One classmate dubbed my writing "The COVID Collection," and someone else suggested it was "Pandemic Poetry," hence the title of this book. Thanks to both of you!

Interestingly, what started out as an observation of the times and how our daily lives and routines had been severely altered started to change. I began to take a turn in tone when, by May, I realized my dissatisfaction with how the Trump administration was not handling and dealing with this health crisis as it had grown. And off I went! I decided to take the summer of '21 off to escape self-imposed pressure to produce on a weekly basis and by the fall, I realized that it was healthier for me not to put so much energy into so many negative thoughts, and I ended my streak.

Now that much of life has begun to resemble the old "normal," I look upon my writings as a journal or documentation of the times and our states of mind, and thought you might enjoy reading the entries, either again, or for the first time. The pandemic is a part of American history which, hopefully, will never be repeated.

COVID Corner

We have a little COVID corner
filled with joys galore:
some face masks and some Clorox wipes
to keep surroundings pure.

Who ever thought we'd love the day
the mailman brought a gift
of sterile gloves and Purell drops
to give our hearts a lift.

New normal has a brand new style --
short on fashion chic
but giving hope of staying well
at least another week!

I long for days of hugs and touch,
free of constraint and fear.
I WILL behave and do things right
to make it through the year.

I know we're very lucky,
our worries are at bay,
but when this damn thing's over-
I'll shout a huge HURRAY!

New Reality Thoughts

My hair's too long, my nails — too short.
There's little pressing to report.
We two are blessed, we're strong of heart.
Our only gripe — to be apart

from grandkids, friends and those most dear.
I hope it's not another year
before we hug or give a kiss.
(There's little else we truly miss!)

We've learned our needs are really small.
The frills of life don't count at all.
Each day's our gift — a chance to live
each moment — water through a sieve.

Our time is precious, we can see
that "someday" may not come to be.
So, love the sun, embrace the gloom
(Thank heavens we've been graced with ZOOM!)

And carry on! We'll muddle through,
avoiding Lysol or the flu!
Who knows just what tomorrow brings.
For now, "Just listen," my heart sings.

Changing Times

I never thought we'd see the day
when "normal" simply went away.
We took for granted where we'd go
without a care, no need to know

if we'd be safe and free from fear
of catching Covid — "Is it near?"
It seems our needs were always met --
a haircut now, a book to get

from local libe, but wait — not open.
(Avoiding Amazon I was hopin'.)
I sit now at home — a day filled with gloom,
it feels like I'm waiting for life to resume.

But life DOES go on, no matter the date
though many activities simply must wait.
We do what we can and we learn to make do.
We search now for joy in little things, true.

The song of a bird, the tint of a flower.
(Aroma of coffee has grown in its power!)
All senses awaken with more time to spare.
I've "stopped to smell roses" and see what is where.

Our lives have slowed down, our rhythms are new.
A chance to see life from a different view.

Present

We thought we could tell
how our days would unfold,
our plans for tomorrow quite certain and bold.
We "knew" what we'd do, the places we'd go
with never a doubt it would really be so.

We took much for granted, assuming the best
but really, we hoped and we planned and we guessed
with no guarantees, but based on convention
assuming fruition of every intention.

We're finding that "now" is all that we've got.
('Twas always the case, in case you forgot!)
We've never been able to plan and be sure
naively expecting for each ill a cure!

But now we must learn to "go with the flow"
accepting each day, while striving to know
the worth of the present, the "now" and the "here."
It's life as we know it, each moment's quite dear.

Remember?

Do you remember the past good old days
of smog from emissions and sight-blinding haze?
When gas was expensive and traffic stood still
and one could use money at the grocery store till?

When people in markets pushed past you for bread,
not caring how closely they came near your head?
We paid no attention to where we would walk,
no arrows to follow as produce we'd stalk.

All shelves were abundant with pork and with beef.
No TP for purchase? Not part of our grief!
Seems folks now are nice, they don't push and shove.
While sporting a face mask or maybe a glove.

Our attitude's shifted as time's not as tight.
We have little choice but to do what is right.
We're locked down at home staying safe from disease
as we know we can't always do as we please.

We long for that day when our fears will subside.
From threatening viruses we will not hide.
One day at a time but hopeful that soon
some wisdom will surface and genius will bloom.

Old Normal

Isn't it funny to turn on TV
and look at commercials with what used to be:
people in restaurants, crowds at a game,
life in "old normal," an era quite tame.

No one wore face masks, they held hands and kissed —
such carefree behavior is something now missed.
No thought was given, 'twas no social distance,
being together would meet no resistance.

We often washed hands if we thought it was needed
because they looked dirty. No warnings were heeded.
Our ways are now different, restrictive and stern,
and if we are smart, we're open to learn

by heeding advice, for science knows best.
The only solution? It's test, test, test, test!
But just as important, we need to adjust
our wants for the future, it's really a must.

We'll never go back, nor should we aspire
to live as we have without the desire
to make our world better, to open our souls,
to honor all beings, regardless their roles.

We are all connected, the choice now is ours
to change our tomorrows and aim for the stars.

"Open"

Will we be safe? It's so hard to know
if venturing forth is the wise way to go.
All states are now "open," "we're back now" it's said.
It doesn't feel right and I'm sensing dread.

We're not heeding science -- it's pushed to the side.
Commerce and politics now lead our ride.
Most guidelines -- not followed, suggestions -- not heeded
to distance or honor that masks still are needed.

So many suffer with incomes aborted.
"Can't shelter forever" -- It's not what doc ordered!
I feel like we're circling but not coming near.
There's chaos, not order and that fuels my fear.

Too little, too late, it's just fits and starts.
The absence of wisdom concerns many hearts.
It's action through planning that can bring relief,
but rushing *sans* knowledge will lead to more grief.

Nothing has changed except cases grow.
Saying "It's over" does not make it so!

Change

So many aspects have led to the woes
we're feeling today. We stand in the throes
of protest and illness, leaders unsound,
violence, frustration — big problems abound.

We're looking for change to undo all that's wrong.
Injustice has reigned, as we know, far too long.
We've taken for granted the freedom of whites
that Blacks do not know, denied of their rights:

living while Black without fear or hate —
a new way of being, a world they await.
I cannot imagine the rage Blacks have known.
They're not seen as equals, our history has shown.

My heart feels such sorrow, I'm willing to do
whatever it takes to bring light into view.
"No justice, no peace," — new attitudes needed.
We cannot rest easy 'til all cries are heeded.

If these words resonated with you, you might want to listen to Brené Brown's podcast "Unlocking Us" as she interviews Professor Ibram X. Kendi, or read his book "How to Be an Antiracist." Also check out The Atlantic website for his June 1st article "The American Nightmare."

"Those who tolerate racism perpetuate racism."
— Representative Al Green, Texas

Dumb

Is it just me or have you noticed, too:
the federal government's bid an adieu
to the ongoing crisis -- it's just not their care,
avoiding discussions. "It's no longer there."

The focus has changed to the coming election.
"Our economy's booming -- soon will be perfection!"
Disease has diminished (not really, but said),
most jobs are returning (again, we're misled).

Distortion abounds and reality's skewed
for the sake of an ego, and we're really screwed!
I don't understand it, it doesn't make sense
that people ignore the first line of defense.

The doctors have proven that masks can save lives.
Defying these orders? I break out in hives!
It isn't a hoax, there's truth and there's reason,
we've got to behave to avert "COVID Season."

Germs do not know color -- no red and no blue.
Making this difference -- it's now up to you.
The folks who won't listen are asking for pain.
I view their defiance with total disdain.

The smart will survive, the dumb likely perish.
I guess they've confirmed that their lives they don't cherish.

Truth

It's deeply disturbing that science is scrapped.
Reality has been forsaken.
It's easy to say that no cases exist
if temperature hasn't been taken.

"Slow down the testing, please!" (actual quote)
The numbers are looking too high.
We know how he counts — he's proved before.
His truth is but one great big lie!

"We all have a right to particular views
but not to one's own set of facts." *
Our country can't thrive if attention's not paid
to what's needed, We mustn't heed hacks

who follow the lead of distortion, deceit
to further the goal of election.
The country's at risk of additional grief.
What's needed — a huge course correction.

"Make sure I win" is a plea that was made
to assure his success in November.
He names flaws in others which really are his.
I long for the days I remember

of leadership wise, of presidents sane,
of strength, wisdom and caring,
to know that our country is safe and secure.
Let's vow that's the purpose we're sharing.

It's not red or blue, but rather what's true
that should motivate how we are living.
Forget party lines and lead with the heart
for a life filled with love and forgiving.

* Daniel Patrick Moynihan

IN THE PAST SEVERAL WEEKS, MY WRITING HAS BEEN INSPIRED BY THE EVENTS OF the times — COVID, protests and the turmoil of the current administration. I've shared my writing not only with you, but hundreds of high school classmates who were recently re-connected by email when the pandemic started. Monday, I learned that my best high school friend, Kathy, with whom I had lost contact after high school, had lost her battle with Parkinson's, and the emails flew fast and furiously in sweet remembrance and melancholy. Hence, the following from me --

Celebrate!

Sitting on a covered porch
Watching summer showers,
I call to mind our youthful days
of carefree joys and powers.

We take for granted endless life
when we are in our prime,
assuming that forever's ours,
no limit to our time.

We learn, as years go flowing by
we can't "rewind," "replay"
the passage of our lives on earth.
We must use every day

to find the beauty and the worth
of precious time we're given.
Connect with what inspires us,
let somber thoughts be driven

from minds and hearts. Instead, rejoice
and honor what is dear.
Connect with friends and those we love
and raise a glass of cheer.

Let's hope for happy times ahead.
There's much we can create.
The clouds will part, the sun will shine.
Life's ours to celebrate!

Lessons

When I was young I used to think that life was always fair,
that we would get what we deserved, no reason for despair.
But now I know that's not the case, it simply isn't true;
and so I face reality seen from a different view.

When things in life don't go as planned, I try to find a meaning,
to make some sense of pain and strife. What reason am I gleaning?
What are the lessons to be learned as history we are living?
What will we feel and take to heart from what these days are giving?

To be alive, to cherish breath, to value every day,
to know that what we've done without can simply go away
yet leave us whole and quite complete. The frills are window dressing.
To see our lives for what they are -- I call that quite a blessing.

Science

Respect for intelligence, lacking so sorely,
is largely the reason we're doing so poorly!
"Guidelines too tough" -- Those words he did utter
for opening schools (so foolish, I shudder).

We're losing this battle I sadly do fear.
We never thought April would come twice this year!
Supplies now are dwindling, the tests are too slow.
It takes much too long to know which way to go.

The "red states" where fools rushed to open too early
insured that they'd fail, protestors so surly.
Egged on by the Prez, the famed "genius stable."
Too many surged forward -- I wish they were able

To listen to Fauci whose wisdom abounds.
Now Trump has ignored him, based on the grounds
"A nice man, it's true but he has made mistakes"!
We're desperate for science now, raising the stakes

for those who ignore him, they're tempting the fates.
We're doomed to lose ground, increasing case rates.

Selfish

I try not to grumble, lament and bemoan
those people whose thinking is not like my own.
It's hard, though, accepting the bliss of not knowing
while many more die and the numbers keep growing.

Science rings true, while protests are hollow.
When leadership fails, no models to follow.
Yes, freedom's important but so is the care
of others, respectful. There's no need to share

the blight of Corona, the mask-less defiant,
with love just for self, rebellion-reliant.
If they choose to perish, it's their choice to make.
But don't wipe out thousands who fall in their wake.

"Insanity is doing the same thing over and over and expecting different results." — Albert Einstein

I guess part of my insanity in these times is that I keep hoping to see a change in how we are dealing with issues at hand. Also hoping you are all well and cheery (that might be easier to accomplish). — B.H.

Learning?

We're meant to learn, as time goes by,
from our mistakes so we can try
to get it right the next time 'round
and use the wisdom that we've found.

I scratch my head with wonder deep
that sadly we've not learned to keep
the knowledge of what's needed now
to fight this virus. We know how

to minimize the threat of death
yet many dare to take each breath
without a mask or social distance,
showing up with great resistance.

Hacks who claim that they know best
do not respect a science test,
yet, all the while they turn deaf ears
preventing progress, causing fears.

Until we learn to use good sense,
which proves just what's our best defense,
we're doomed. Mistakes of mindless dolts
will only bring the same results.

Inspiration

We've been away for several days
sans paper and TV,
and with the absence of those "thorns"
I've learned a bit 'bout me.

My anger levels have declined,
my ire has calmed, it's true.
And so I thought I'd share this fact,
perhaps you know it, too.

I rant and rave, I curse the screen,
the headlines knot my gut.
The shame of what's NOT happening
has put me in a rut.

I look for chances to relax,
to sigh with great relief.
'Tis better to connect with thoughts
that do not bring me grief.

And while the views from "paradise"
bring comfort for a while,
we must accept reality
and not live in denial.

Continued

The angst and frowns cause little change,
except they do remind us
we can't forget all those in pain
and put their grief behind us.

Through diligence and change we sow,
encouraging a course
that makes a difference in our world --
I'll shout 'til I am hoarse:

treat all mankind with dignity
(we're cut from cloth the same).
Consider EVERY person's plight.
I do not need to name

the need for freedom and respect,
for basic human rights.
We can't resist because we're fine,
we must uphold the fights

to bring on change, inspired by those
who never stopped believing.
We CAN succeed where there's a will.
'Til then, my heart keeps grieving.

Hopeful

I didn't know just what I'd write.
My spirits were quite low.
It felt like we were stuck in mud.
The day was dreary, slow.

Yes, still no changes to our fix —
our science still not heeded.
I hoped that I would be inspired.
Good news was what I needed.

And then I heard of Biden's choice.
It felt like fog had lifted.
Ms. Harris is a ray of sun.
I think we have been gifted.

This woman is a splendid choice.
She'll surely change the scene.
She's smart, she's sharp and adds so much.
I'm really very keen

to see how Joe's campaign will thrive.
The ticket's face she's changed.
Diversity, experience.
Perhaps life's rearranged!

Scary Times

I've lately been tempted to rant and to rave --
(behavior, I know, unbecoming)!
I feel great frustration at efforts displayed
to upend the election upcoming.

I don't know what happened to honor and truth,
for winning a vote fair and square,
to seeking an office with merit, not lies,
it leads me to feel great despair.

A long time ago, I'd no interest in news,
I buried my head in the sand,
believing it didn't connect with my life,
I just didn't understand.

But then I got "woke" and found that I cared
and knew that I had to give voice.
With SO much corruption in politics now,
there's need for a powerful choice.

I never liked politics, much like Michelle,
yet cared very deeply for rights.
Knowing "democracy now is at stake"*
my inner voice calls out for fights

To stand up to tyranny, eyes opened wide.
We can't have an emperor or tsar.
Ignoring our roles to defend freedom's needs
will certainly not take us far

Continued

*Sally Yates, former U.S. Deputy Attorney General

From all we detest, like children in cages,
denial of rights, rules of law.
By NOT standing up to that we're against,
we're saying it's something we're for.

These times are quite scary, think Germany '40s,
when power grew, snakelike and quiet.
Could happen again, unless we're prepared.
I don't want to wake to a riot

that follows election, if Mr. B wins.
We know T has threatened he'll stay
regardless of outcome, he'll call it a hoax.
(Truth never did get in his way!)

So, speak up, be counted and follow a path
that leads us to where we must be,
with honor and caring for everyone's life.
It's now up to you and to me.

Ponderings

I don't have a problem with diff'ring opinions.
Our parties don't usually see eye to eye.
What DOES drive me crazy is prevarication.
Freedom of speech isn't freedom to lie.

I'm also quite troubled by character failure --
the lack of conviction, integrity, guts.
Selling one's soul to assure reelection
is very pathetic, if not simply nuts.

I never cared much for political struggles,
Naively believing that all would be fine.
But now it is crucial with power abuse.
Democracy's neck seems to be on the line.

We don't need an emperor, dictator, tyrant,
permanent leader or even a king.
Yet that looks to be the direction we're headed.
I hope we'll wake up so that freedom can ring!

LAST YEAR, CHUCK AND I HAPPENED TO TUNE IN TO A PBS PROGRAM THAT featured an interview with Timothy Snyder, a history professor at Yale. In 2017 he wrote a small and powerful book titled "On Tyranny: Twenty Lessons from the Twentieth Century." It's a quick read and VERY important. If you haven't already seen it, you might want to take a look at it. Most of us have heard that our president has great admiration for despots, and this book is an eye opener as to how a country goes from being a democracy to a fascist state. Many of us were very young, if even alive, when Hitler rose to power, and Snyder's observations may give you pause.

Conventions

I will not be snarky, I will not be mean
as I contrast the recent conventions we've seen.
One was quite hopeful, in praising diversity.
T'other bore forecast of total adversity.

Future with promise and praise of man's worth
or threats of catastrophe, "end of the earth!"
Folks speaking gently with voices quite calm
or yelling and screaming as shrill as a bomb!

One was quite forthright with plans for success,
the other spawned fiction, bombastic distress!
One followed protocol, respecting tradition,
the other — law breaking and blind with ambition.

One group was distanced, avoiding congestion.
The other ignored scientific suggestion.
Leadership passionate, caring with soul,
endeavoring to make this America whole.

Revisionist history, eager to blame
an alternate reality, grifting with shame.
I hope that Americans take off their blinders,
respecting our forefathers' thoughtful reminders.

See with clear vision the choices at hand,
preserving integrity throughout this land.

O N THIS DAY OF REMEMBRANCE, I AM TAKING A MOMENT TO RECALL *ALL* THE dear ones who have brought me joy. In these strange and challenging times it's easy, isn't it, to focus on things we miss or what's different or even annoying. (I know I grumble about the political scene and worry about our environment.) But at the same time, I must try to remember to take a step back and realign my vision to appreciate all that's available and joyful.

Joy

I choose to make each moment count,
to find the joy in smallest treasures.
Things we often took for granted
now become a source of pleasures.

Cloudless skies and grandkids' voices,
a rosy perfect summer peach.
No need to travel far and wide --
these treats are all within our reach!

'Stead of ruing what we're missing,
notice what is close at hand.
Fabled glass CAN be half full
if we will let our minds expand.

Tune in, focus, see surroundings,
opened eyes -- the joys are there.
Yes, the world can lift your spirits.
Seek and you will find your share.

Aware

When life is politicized, COVID called "hoax,"
sorry's the state of those misinformed folks.
When truth is rejiggered (political need)
and science rewritten to match faulty screed,

we must blow the whistle and end this deceit,
for lives are in danger from one man's conceit.
There's too much at stake to remain calmly silent.
Our job — raise awareness to fight all that's violent.

Dear Dr. Fauci, I hope that your voice
will offer persuasion for each voter's choice.
Despite his awareness that danger was there
Trump maintained a silence, the market to spare.

His thought — reelection — his only concern,
defiant of science, refusing to learn.
His rallies are risky — no masks and no space,
(a surefire method to wipe out his base!)

Refuting the fact that it's gonna get worse.
He doesn't protect and his words are a curse!
Ignoring the truth, denying the facts,
he threatens young lives, repeating his hacks.

I hope that our country will notice and heed
the good information that all of us need
to outlive this threat, come through it and thrive.
If not for his sins, many more'd be alive!

WE LOST A GIANT ON FRIDAY, DESPITE HER DIMIN-
utive physical stature. An amazing force, she has and
will continue to inspire people for decades to come.

RBG

She was our rudder, our touchstone of wisdom,
endlessly fighting for all that was fair.
Guiding us forward through turbulent waters,
it's hard to accept that she's no longer there.

Heavy's my heart as I think of the changes
that threaten our future at this point in time,
so many freedoms that soon may be stolen.
Stressful, for sure, this political clime!

Science is altered and rights now in question,
healthcare and climate at risk of defeat.
We are at war to maintain what she fought for.
Can't turn our heads -- we must rise up to meet

the challenges looming. I fear for reversal
of all that was won which allowed us some choice.
I want to be hopeful and not churn with worry.
I'm longing to hear a new leadership voice.

"King"

There once was a man who thought he was king,
mimicking despots who made his heart sing.
He craved big displays of parades filled with tanks
to honor his being, his ego (no thanks!).

Surrounded by cronies, the ones with big bucks,
he did as he wanted, not giving two f*cks!
He worshipped his daughter, his sons not so much,
while endlessly boasting of his Midas Touch!

Convinced he'd continue for year after year,
he paid no attention, refusing to hear
the voice of the people who said, "Don't appoint
'til after election" but he'd self-anoint.

He scorned our traditions and scoffed at all laws.
His reckless behavior gave reason for pause.
He earned while presiding, paid such minor taxes,
he ruined our standing among worldwide axis.

All that he did was with one thing in mind —
to serve his own pleasure, contempt for mankind.
One only could hope that his reign soon would end
so wisdom and honor would be our new trend.

PERHAPS YOU'VE COME TO REALIZE, AS WE HAVE, THAT THE PEOPLE OUTSIDE OUR home to whom we say "thank you" are those who don't have the luxury of staying home, away from potential COVID harm. More than ever, it's so important to express our gratitude for the work they are doing to make our lives easier.

Smiles

It's come to my attention
that we are smile-deprived.
By wearing masks we cover up
the way our thanks have thrived.

When acts of kindness came my way
I'd often flash a grin.
But now I've come to realize
it's covered, nose to chin.

So now we must engage our words
'cause eyes don't say enough.
Call up those words of gratitude
expressing thanks -- not tough!

Sunshine

I wish I could bottle a day like today —
the pure, brilliant sunlight, caresses of breezes.
I'd save it for winter when days will be short.
The darkness will call out for something that pleases.

I wish I could capture the song of the bird,
the glow of the foliage, the crispness of air,
to hear and to feel the delights of this day,
to counter the gloom of winter's despair.

When first we begin to stay close to our nests,
the days started growing and earth sprang to bloom.
I wonder what goodness the winter will bring
to offer a respite from days dark with gloom.

Note to myself: Stay present, don't fret.
Yes, we will move forward to gray days ahead.
I'll treasure my sunshine and smile at my mem'ries.
The beauty of snowfalls will soon fill my head!

TRY AS I MIGHT TO KEEP IT LIGHT, I CAN'T GET away from my irritation at what could have been a very different scenario. Hope you are all well and not pandemic-fatigued. Don't let your guards down!

Observations

Like dogs wearing muzzles and horses with feedbags,
mankind looks different with masks on our faces.
So much has changed in our daily routines,
wherever we go, maintaining our spaces.

One year ago if I'd ventured a guess
as to what would be hot and in great demand,
it wouldn't be Plexiglass, Purell or wipes
that would rise to the top of the "musts" near at hand.

I might have had gripes about government actions
pertaining to tax breaks or maybe the clime.
But now it is COVID, completely unmanaged,
that occupies thought so much of the time.

We have been robbed of a chance to be joyful
or mournful together, with passage of rites.
It needn't have been, if more care had been taken
and warnings were heeded, but such was the might

of a self-centered "ruler" who cares not for others.
Incompetence put us in front of harm's way.
There's no turning back now -- we only look forward
to ending his power. I long for that day!

DEAR FRIENDS AND FAMILY, AS I MAY HAVE TOLD YOU, MY WEEKLY POEM POSTings began shortly after the outbreak of COVID. A high school classmate had emailed 120 of us to say he hoped we were all well and that he had been washing his hands so frequently that he finally uncovered the answers to the social studies quiz! Many responded to his humor and reached out to others. That's just around the time I wrote my first pandemic poem, and I decided to share it with my class, with whom I had not been in touch for many, many years. And I heard from SO many people from my past, encouraging me to keep going.

In the beginning, I simply observed all the life changes we shared. But as the pandemic continued, I began to realize that our government was not responding promptly or adequately, and that's when my tone changed and I couldn't remain silent. Twice I invited my classmates to opt out of receiving my biting verse, but out of 120 names, only four people asked to be removed from my weekly mailings. I am assuming that most if not all of you are on the same page as I am. If you want to opt out, please feel free if we don't see eye to eye. Otherwise, here is my most impassioned musing to date. Please feel free to share it.

Because both presidential candidates are so diametrically opposed not only politically but even more so morally, many families as well as friends are at odds as they choose their candidate.

Our upcoming election is life-changing; it will affect the quality of our existence for decades to come. Especially in these extraordinary times, your vote is an indication of who you are, your values, your ethics and your moral compass. A vote for Trump is a vote for autocracy, voter suppression, child abuse, racism, bigotry, denial of science, dishonesty and his misogynistic tendencies. A vote for Trump is a stamp of approval for continuing these travesties.

A Plea

As E-day draws closer, I'm very on edge,
concerned that democracy sways on a ledge
where balance can totter and truth takes a dive.
Without course correction, we cannot survive.

Please make your choice, not by thinking of taxes,
kowtowing to lobbies, integrity lapses.
Consider the future, our children and "grands,"
protecting a country where liberty stands.

We all want what's best, but how does that look?
(Deception, autocracy? Not in my book!)
Honor is missing and courage to act
with forthright conviction, according to fact.

There's so much at stake, as we make our selection
to safeguard democracy in this election.
Please value our essence and choose whom you trust.
To safeguard this nation, smart voting's a must!

Waiting

"Remember to breathe, drop shoulders from ears."
(Reminders to me to allay baseless fears!).
My heart's in my throat, my stomach — a knot!
I'll try to stay hopeful. It's all that I've got.

The voting is over, the ballots all cast,
awaiting an outcome. Decisions at last!
Yes, voting has stopped but counting has not,
so patience is needed to sweeten the pot.

The Buddhists suggest we release any plans,
accepting, instead, what future commands.
That's all well and good, but still takes a toll,
not knowing's a challenge and tough on one's soul!

I hope that no effort to dodge a defeat
will cause anyone to resort to deceit!
A win — fair and square — the wish that we hold —
a prez with integrity, honest and bold.

Optimism

It's now just beginning, with hard work ahead,
with healing, uniting, without sense of dread.
The people have spoken, they've chosen a man
who cares -- empathetic -- the start of a plan

to listen to science, to lead with a heart,
to work for all people, not tear them apart.
I'll no longer cringe when the president speaks.
I know that our leaders will summit high peaks.

We'll retake the planet and plan for survival
with no more destruction -- a chance for revival.
A sense, now, of decency flows in our veins.
Though much has been lost, there's a plan, now, for gains.

In fighting disease, supporting the needy,
not simply rewarding those swamp beasts so greedy!
With damage reversal and many repairs
we WILL build back better, with far fewer cares.

Trumpty*

Trumpty Dumpty sat on a wall.
(Wouldn't you think he'd know he might fall?)
He DID fall apart as he crashed to the ground
but wouldn't acknowledge the mess all around!

The people who saw him said, "My, he's undone
and even his orange is starting to run!"
But Trumpty heard nothing, insisting "No break!"
Demanding a redo, his ego a-quake!

Acknowledging breakage -- he just couldn't do it.
Best buddies saw nothing -- thus, just no truth to it!
The ones seeing clearly could see he was broken
and talk of repair would merely be token.

The mess that he made he refused to repair.
He just left the scene with nary a care.
He seems to be hiding, avoiding display,
but insiders say he's now feeling dismay.

Though time to move forward, he's stuck in his tracks,
not caring for others, he's called upon quacks
Agreeing "no problem, let things run the course.
Ignore it, no need now for governing force."

If only he'd leave, letting others begin
the work that's required, our battles to win.
While he is around, he impedes course correction.
It's time we move on in a different direction.

*Title credit to John Lithgow for the name "Trumpty"

Gratitude

I had planned to take a break,
to spare your eyes/my mind from rhyme.
But words and thoughts came flooding in
as we approach this festive time.

This has been a different year
with many "don'ts," behaviors new.
But most of what we've done without
is minor, with exceptions few.

I pause to reevaluate
what I have done and what I treasure.
Living in a different way
has brought some unexpected pleasure.

New behavior, new adventures,
viewing life with new perspective,
staying present, in the moment,
focusing on a new directive.

Giving thanks, a daily pause,
refreshes, pushing clouds away.
In these times that challenge life
I'm grateful now for every day.

Upset

I'd love to be upbeat and quick to rejoice
the excellent folks who are now Biden's choice.
But so much is frightful, the world has gone mad
with actions that leave me quite worried and sad.

The world keeps on turning, despite my chagrin
with daily occurrences — where to begin?
We had an election — 'twas deemed fair and square
yet half of our country denies Biden's there.

With calls now for murder, requests for a hanging
of government workers besieged with haranguing
because they were truthful, reflecting the voice
of voters for Biden, quite clear in their choice.

"No fraud," spoke Sir Barr but Trump won't accept,
while proving again that he's totally inept,
like a king whose gone mad with "I won, yes, I won!"
It seems that he's lost it — a party of one.

What bothers me, though, are the silent Repubs
who slunk and sit huddling like tiny bear cubs
afraid to state truth because of HIS might.
What happened to honesty, dignity, "right"?

Family pardons, and talk of no show
when Biden's sworn in — what a low way to go.
Trump's proved no morals, inciting ill will.
The truth, we can say, is a tough, bitter pill.

Truth/Reality

It seems that reality no longer counts.
Election results were rejected
by losers accustomed to getting their way,
refusing the truth they expected.

Instead they invented their own set of facts,
creating an alternate fiction
not found anywhere on library shelves.
It's become a new form of addiction:

appeasing the emperor wearing no clothes,
the safe way to stay in his graces.
It's sad they've no vision, cajoled by his threats.
He's certainly put them through paces.

I get that the henchmen must tiptoe around.
They mustn't admit to the truth.
But what of the millions across our great land
drinking Kool-Aid or is it vermouth?

The people in charge who are doing their jobs,
regardless of whom they support,
at least show some spine, refusing to cave
(and winning their cases in court).

I hope there's a way for the truth to prevail
despite all attempts of denial.
We must not have coups to settle disputes.
Democracy CAN'T be on trial!

Joyful?

It's hard to be joyful with news of unrest,
and while I continue to hope for the best,
our country's at war, right here on our land
as protests rise up with malice at hand.

Refusing acceptance that Biden has won,
the Proud Boys and others choose violence (their fun!),
denying the truth, defying the facts,
democracy's threatened by small-minded hacks.

It's shameful, the actions of people elected
to serve us in Congress. Who could have expected
they'd forsake the vows they swore to uphold.
Instead, serving Trump — it's treason untold.

They're blinded by greed, in fear of his power,
they're showing true colors, like cowards they cower.
Integrity's gone, heartbreaking to see.
Encouraged by Trump, disruptions flow free.

It's hard to believe we've devolved to this state.
Let's hope we'll rebound with a chance to be great.

FA-LA-LA

'Tis the day before Christmas and all through the House
and Senate, it's quiet -- not even a mouse.
The members of Congress have all gone away
to celebrate Christmas, light-hearted and gay.

I'm glad that they voted (too late, just a start),
a token, perhaps, meant to lighten one's heart.
But what of the millions with sorrows and woes
that stem from our tragedy, deep in the throes

of poverty, joblessness, truly unable
to make the next rent or put food on the table.
Where is compassion and care for our brothers?
I sometimes believe we've forgotten the others

less lucky or skillful or born of a color
that heightens their plight just to live like another.
This holiday season, intensify caring
by giving and thinking, loving and sharing.

Happier New Year!

We wind down a year that we never expected
and hope for a new year, most problems corrected.
We've suffered great sorrows with fear and with strife
from businesses closing to huge loss of life.

Our children were cheated of school as we knew it
and millions lost jobs — "How would they get through it?"
Our normal has morphed and we've had to adjust
with far fewer frills but reason to trust.

Precautions will keep us from threatening ills.
Surviving's more valid than quick, fleeting thrills.
It's time to look forward to sunnier days
with promise of healing in so many ways.

The hope that our science will thwart more disease
and life will rebound, with far greater ease.
It may take some time to feel free of stress.
Just when will it happen? It's anyone's guess!

P.S. My husband, Chuck, answers that last question:
"Vaccines are coming and Trump's going!"

Relief?

When Wednesday began, I felt lightness of heart
for Georgia's election foretold a fresh start:
a page has been turned, most roadblocks removed.
Let's hope that the passage of laws is improved.

"Grim reaper" soon gone, not blocking the way,
the Senate will function, both sides having "say."
We heave a collective sigh of relief,
secure in the knowledge we're ending the grief

of standstills and willful obstruction of care
for many in need, now ending despair.
As Wednesday unfolded, 'twas lawless direction
encouraged by Trump -- indeed, insurrection.

I'm mournful and angry -- all caused by deceit
by those saying Trump never suffered defeat,
With lie after lie, no proof of votes stolen.
(this fable created for his ego swollen.)

It's horrid, the riots, the chaos, sedition,
incited by those who are doomed to perdition!
This vile siege of terror should end in arrest
of ALL the inciters, the Prez and the rest.

We need to be rid of this despot so craven.
I'm counting the days 'til we reach a safe haven.

Lies

Neo-Nazis, QAnon,
bigots, racists, on and on.
These "loved" folks obeyed the urge
from Prez (the Don) so he could purge

all those who aren't Aryan white,
with Rudy, Junior, pressing might.
The first **Big Lie** was years ago —
his oath of office? T'wasn't so!

No love of country, ego fed
to boost his brand, that's how he "led."
Then "Voter Fraud" — **Lie number 2** —
So oft repeated, some thought true.

His tactic used, we have observed,
promoting lies. I'm quite unnerved
that so many follow blind and willing.
"Alternative truth" is quite blood-chilling.

Lie Number 3 — "Antifa caused
Jan. 6 uprising" gives me pause.
I'm tired of the violence,
the grift and the graft.

It's time to move on.
Our country's gone daft.

Fresh Start

I send prayers of safety for all those attending
Joe Biden's big shindig as Trump's reign is ending.
While we can rejoice that we'll have a fresh start
with capable leaders, experienced and smart,

there's still a huge problem that won't go away
until truth is heeded, myths no more in play.
The sale of the BIG LIE -- that Trump truly won --
commenced 2016, his plan had begun.

The cult who believed him were led by the nose,
ignoring the facts in exchange for sales prose.
For him, down was up and white really black.
He kept on misleading, promoting his hack

that no one but he really dealt in the truth,
his sycophants fawning in ways so uncouth
'til facts didn't matter, their world became altered.
Reality weakened, democracy faltered.

The pity today -- so many are blind.
A modern-day fascist has captured each mind
of those who believe that Joe Biden's not chief.
Our country must rise to abolish belief

of rubbish and rot from the Kool-Aid they drank.
They think they're so smart but, in fact, to be frank,
they demonstrate weakness, they're led by the nose
refusing the truth -- they're dumb and it shows!

I hope, as time passes, as Biden will show
his leadership's sound and we'll all feel a glow
with knowledge that we will bounce back, not all lost.
And keep moving forward, no matter the cost.

Relief

Like so many friends who value the truth
we've heaved a collective sigh —
relieved that disaster is not looming near.
Integrity reigning on high!

Though much is required of our Prez and our Veep,
we know their intentions to lead
will come from the heart. Respect for the law
shall guide how they govern — not greed!

The world keeps on spinning despite our restrictions.
We distance, we mask and wash hands.
We've formed these new habits. They're now automatic,
accepting our new life's demands.

Let's picture a day when these woes are behind us,
the threat of Corona long past.
It's up to us all to follow the call
to ensure this condition won't last.

Addiction

Members of a certain party
suffer from a grave affliction.
Loss of spine is one such symptom
of what is known as "Trump Addiction!"

Stockholm Syndrome, to be sure,
they've learned to love the one who "deals,"
spreading lies and spreading fear.
Though out of office, he still appeals

to those who fear he'll shoot them down.
They cower, lest they cause him rage.
Their love of country, lost to love
of his support. They're in a cage!

They're trapped, afraid to speak the truth,
Afraid the power that THEY'VE given
will be used against their seats
and from their jobs they will be driven.

Shame on those who've lost the truth
with actions and with words outrageous.
They've left what's real, they pander and bow.
Trump's lies, I guess, are quite contagious.

Lives were lost because of lies.
Extremists rallied, cowards rose
to please their prez and "stop the steal."
We need them caught -- their treason shows!

Babble!

Happy Valentine's Day!

I'm deeply fatigued, disgusted and weary
with babbling efforts to undo a claim
that one former leader directed a riot
and caused loss of life, denying his blame.

If t'weren't so serious, it would be comical,
watching his sycophants (blind to the truth)
declare "Let's move on -- it's time now for unity!"
Their only concern is the next voting booth.

The hair-splitting verbiage of those who defend him
is so far afield of what's really at stake:
respect for democracy, love of our country.
Their efforts to heal are nothing but fake!

Change

I pinch myself, I'm filled with joy.
We've left the twilight zone!
We have a prez who acts like one,
Our leader's changed the tone.

Transparency has now arrived.
We know what's going on.
No impulse law, no vengeful acts,
the daily fear is gone.

Docs speaking freely words of truth.
We'll know where problems lie
and rise to meet those challenges.
The truth they won't deny.

Soon shots in arms and checks in pockets,
we'll feel that change can flourish.
Approvals high with care for all,
this prez knows how to nourish!

Unknowns

I so often wonder just how it will feel
when COVID's behind us and life's less restrictive.
Will masks become obsolete, distancing stopped
and hand washing maybe a bit less addictive?

We'll go where we want, eat out on a whim,
behave rather casually, perhaps worry-free.
Attend shows and concerts, and celebrate travel
and visits with friends to a greater degree.

But what of the businesses shuttered and closed?
Will they have a chance to return to their norms?
Can they see a rebirth, regain what has perished,
rebound from the depths, surviving life's storms?

And what of the children who've lost so much time
with teachers and friends, their innocence bruised?
How will this disturbance leave marks on their psyches,
their learning disrupted, their "normal" abused?

There are no instructions for life in the future.
We'll learn as we go, exploring new ways
to cope with unknowns and hope we've gained knowledge,
creating successes and happier days.

The Orange God-King

The Orange God-King still insists
he won the last election.
He rants and raves, his Big Lie thrives,
some cited for "defection."

I'd really hoped he'd fade away
like other "formers" -- quiet.
He fans the flames, inciting base
and won't condemn the riot.

No Senate Rep would vote "impeach."
Such cowards, they were fearful.
Quoting technicalities,
Mitch gave us quite an earful.

Now Switch-Pitch Mitch, a hypocrite
with memory quite failing,
Will fall in line in '24
to save his neck from flailing!

Relief II

Those whose thinking matches mine
know there's cause for celebration.
Bucks will soon be on their way
for those who suffer in our nation.

Most (or all) who read my musings
have not ailed or gone the way
of many, losing jobs or lives,
enduring pain most every day.

Yet, I wonder, why the struggle?
Why can't Reps show heart and caring?
Digging in, on party lines,
makes little sense and is quite wearing.

Polls have shown that more than half
our population wants this aid.
Yet the Senate is the scene
of single-minded Red charade.

Voting While Black?

While I take great comfort with Dems at the helm,
I'm struck with a new form of fear.
Voter suppression's a hideous crime,
removing a privilege quite dear

From people whose voices must surely be heard —
less "worthy," ignored or berated.
The obstacles some chose to place in their way
are sadly anticipated.

The Reps know they're losers if voting is held
in a manner both fair and inclusive.
They've said it: To garner the "ayes" they would need,
their methods must then be abusive!

Reflecting

Reflecting on the year that's passed,
much is different, much the same.
We've learned how we must make adjustments
all the while we play the game

Of LIFE with all our wants and needs.
We compensate in ways quite new.
We travel less, we nest far more,
finding different pathways to

our end goals — growth and stimulation --
experiences now unfolding,
challenged by the lack of "normal,"
yielding now instead of holding

that which we have always done.
Tasting newness, open hearts,
letting go of same old, same old,
open now to fresh new starts.

Scheming and Scamming

Scheming and scamming, still reaching in pockets
of fans unsuspecting of T's viral lies.
It's shameful his party continues to follow
like members of cults with blinders on eyes.

Sad for naive ones who do not know better,
but what of the others we think of as "smart"?
They act with their egos, in favor of income,
protecting their office, not using their hearts.

Their moral convictions have flown out the window.
They scoff at integrity, choosing instead
to vote with the party that's crumbled to pieces,
their honor and caring are surely quite dead!

Calendar

I used to look forward to calendars bursting --
appointments to keep and places I'd go.
But all that has changed and my days mine to use
in ways quite spontaneous, impromptu and slow.

I called them "look forwards" -- the plans in my date book,
impatient to count down the days that awaited.
Ironic -- I'd find that the actual happening
did not yield the joy I had anticipated.

It's funny, but now I don't think of the future
as something that's better, more pleasant or choice.
I "live in the moment," I savor what's current.
I'm tuned to the present and hearing its voice.

We have just this moment, so make every minute
the best it can be, enjoy here and now.
Drink in what's happening and treasure its richness.
"I'm well and I'm thriving" -- let that be your vow.

Just a Start ...

Accountability was served;
the verdicts handed down.
It's just a start and not a fix.
The problems still abound.

Our country, sadly, harbors hate.
Justice hasn't flourished,
with thousands losing lives and rights.
Reform must now be nourished.

Writing

Some days the words just seem to flow. I barely pause to think
of how I'll share the thoughts I have with paper, pen and ink.
On other days I agonize, my mind seems stuck in mud.
Though always thinking, I will find my thoughts land with a thud!

'Twas easy when the sense of rage provoked by "previous guy"
would cause my words to spew like lava , bubbling toward the sky.
I'm far more calm tho still I bristle with the daily news.
The thought of lost democracy provokes a case of blues.

Suppressing votes or turning backs on need for thoughtful law
still aggravates my sense of calm and tension hits my jaw!
'Twould be far simpler to ignore the trials of daily life
and tune out lest I feel some pain, exposing me to strife.

It's true that blocking out the news is like a brain "vacation."
My need to know is far too great to dodge life's tribulations.
And so I think and growl, then reach for paper, pen and pad.
If I can bring awareness, some good comes from the bad!

Baffled

I just do not get it (I may be naive).
The myths from Republicans -- hard to believe.
Most of the statements most Reps come to utter --
so far from the truth that they cause me to shudder!

Elections of yore, when you won, it was fact.
The loser bowed graciously, not: "We've been hacked!"
And other excuses to back their refusal
to say "Biden won." No, instead, their accusal

that votes had been stolen, the count must be phony!
In truth, their reality's simply baloney!
The few -- Mitt and Liz -- who dare speak the truth
are under attack for their stance so uncouth.

The Reps clearly demonstrate facts no more matter.
Just make up a tale and its seeds soon will scatter,
so more and more people accept the Big Lie.
They hear it so often, in to it they buy.

The Trumpeteer still pulls the strings of the dummies
who follow him blindly with brains more like mummies,
And so we continue, with truth vs. story.
(I never dreamed politics could be so gory!)

Saddened

I'm really quite saddened when hearing the news
that so many people have now come to choose
belief in a party that does not speak truth;
they live in an alternate world, so uncouth.

I fear our democracy teeters and wobbles.
(It's more than just differences, parties with squabbles.)
An effort continues to end voters' rights;
they seem to concoct weak excuses to fight

the means that allow for great numbers to cast
a ballot for justice (a thing of the past?).
Belief in pure witchcraft -- the claim that Trump won,
a sign that deception's already begun.

The cult seems to have but only one aim --
to win, *sans* integrity ... that is their game,
our grandkids soon thrust in a world of deceit.
Protecting democracy -- no easy feat!

Confused

Should we or shouldn't we? That is the task,
determining whether to put on a mask.
We value the science, the leaders and words
put out there to guide us but we don't have herds

to give us immunity, there's still much unknown.
Though case counts have dropped, I can't be alone
in wondering how to protect those not vaxxed --
the little ones, others subject to attacks.

I question the "honor" of those who refuse
to get the vaccines, will they really choose
to mask up with others, it's quite hard to say.
(Tho they are the ones most at risk, end of day.)

We're all very eager to put this behind
and face each new day with great peace of mind
that COVID is over, but can we be sure?
The question still looms 'til we find us a cure.

With varying guidance, I think we must do
what feels most protective from our own point of view.

Chill

I'm suffering from brain freeze —
the words just don't flow.
And while there's so much
that could make my angst grow,

I'm trying to chill and enjoy a great day
devoid of the strife which so oft makes me bray!
So easy 'twould be for me to lament.
Today, tho, I've vowed that my time will be spent

enjoying the moment, concerns pushed aside,
remaining quite present, I'll savor the ride!

Fatigue

Folks are fatigued from following protocols,
keeping their distances, covering faces.
Wanting to put inconvenience behind them,
"COVID is over!" -- they're back to their paces

on beaches, in ballparks -- the crowds overwhelming,
as if there's no threat to our health anymore.
I guess I'm more cautious, proceeding more slowly
yet hopeful that challenges won't be in store.

P.S. Yesterday Dr. Fauci announced, "It's not over yet!"

The Last Elected President?

Will Biden be viewed as our country's last president,
followed by despots, dictators or kings?
The Reps are afraid of each vote being counted
(as crim'nal as those suffering Dante's 9 rings).

The Reps are afraid of elections held fairly.
They're certain to lose and so they react.
The previous election — the one most unhampered —
inspires their need for "Suppress the Vote" acts.

The thought of defeat has been deemed unacceptable,
inspiring behavior that just isn't right.
Democracy teeters, on brink of destruction.
Integrity's called for. We must win this fight!

Reflections

I think of our world a mere year ago,
concerned we'd catch COVID, perhaps knowing fear.
The times now so different, such worries relaxed.
We're safe from those threats, so it would appear.

But new problems haunt us — Democracy's fragile —
for truth and integrity — they're on the wane.
Nefarious actions are now seen as normal.
(Whatever it takes to protect their domain!)

The laws being passed to skew fair elections
are shocking, disgraceful, defying belief.
For justice to serve us, we MUST demand action
lest we are all doomed to a world filled with grief.

Perplexed

I've come to conclude that I don't understand
the minds of many who govern this land.
When I studied Civics — a term now long gone —
we learned certain concepts to govern upon.

We chose reps and senators to speak with OUR voice,
to hear OUR desires and follow OUR choice
for actions of government. They took a vow
to follow their voters, who let them know how

they wanted our country to follow their lead.
Instead, there are many who, hearts filled with greed,
will do as they please, intentions corrupt.
Their aim: Change elections! All rights they disrupt!

They're bigots and racists with hearts full of hate,
ignoring the concepts our founders found great.
Gone is integrity. Win at all cost,
even when counts would appear they had lost!

I'm sad and I'm sickened at how we've devolved.
This problem is huge! How will it be solved?

Brevity

It's beastly hot,
my brain is fried!
I'd hoped to write —
I really tried!

For now I'll chill
and take a break
I'll lighten up!
This vow I'll make!

Dear All,

I hope that those of you dealing with extreme heat are faring well. I wanted to let you all know that I am planning to take a summer sabbatical! If Congress can do it, then so can I, but I'm planning on two months, not one!

When I began my writing, two clever classmates (Ellen and Bill — forgive me if I'm wrong about that) referred to my musings as the COVID Collection of Pandemic Poetry. I was indeed expressing my reactions to our then new life style. I was lighthearted in the beginning but by late Spring I became angry at the realization that the administration wasn't dealing wisely with COVID. By mid-summer, I was terribly concerned that we might see another Trump presidency. At that point I extended an invitation to all of you to "unsubscribe" with no hard feelings, and a few classmates took me up on that. Perhaps you were too polite and instead just chose to dump my weekly writing without reading it!

I don't want to overstay my welcome and frankly I feel as if I need a break from focusing my creative juices on happenings that are so negative. Yes, it's been an outlet for my frustration, but even I think I've been very dark lately. That doesn't mean I will ignore what's going on in our country — we must all be aware — but I need to take a breather with, perhaps, unreasonable faith that the Dems will meet their/our challenges and put an end to so much of the madness in today's government.

And so I wish you all a splendid, healthy summer with more good news to look forward to. Depending on where I am, creatively and emotionally, I may very well either surprise you with an unexpected musing this summer or simply resume with happier thoughts to ponder after the summer.

I am so grateful to all of you who have reached out to me with comments, positive or negative; I've reconnected with many people I completely lost touch with since our last reunion, and it's been an unexpected gift!

Thanks for listening and stay well and happy!

Warmly,
Beth

A Day at a Time

A day at a time —
it's what we must do
as life throws us wrenches
and we muddle through.

Each day a new chance
to do what we can
to help one another,
creating a plan

for life filled with promise,
productive and sharing
that's low in combustion
but high with deep caring.

Our world's upside down
with balance required.
There's so much unrest
that my heart's very tired

of aching for those
who witness such need,
while others with power
think only of greed.

I wish there were more
I could do to improve
the state of our being
and find a new groove.

I long for great changes,
for peace and well-being.
It seems we'll need miracles
to change what we're seeing!

Lies

I thought I'd be able to stifle the urge
to vent my frustrations, my anger to purge.
but since I'm not brain-dead, non-hearing or blind,
I can't help reacting and clearing my mind!

It seems that reality no longer matters --
the lies that we're hearing must come from mad hatters
who make up their stories to change our perception.
The truth? Why, it's gone and we're left with deception.

I'm speechless, but need to describe my reaction.
Will honesty ever regain precious traction?
There's no vax for "evil" -- we must stop this lying.
Dear Dems, please rise up to prevent truth from dying!

WHAT STARTED OUT AS LIGHTHEARTED OBSERVATIONS EVOLVED INTO A SPOT-light on frustrations and sorrows of the past administration as well as hope-fulness that things would soon improve. But times still weigh heavily on me, and I don't want to focus more negative energy on the happenings in our world such as it is today.

I will try to remain upbeat and optimistic, challenging as it is. But I don't think that my poems can necessarily reflect that attitude, so I have, with careful consideration, decided not to resume my weekly postings now that summer is drawing to an end and my "recess" is over.

I hope all of you have been well and will remain so, despite the upsurge of COVID (don't get me started!). I'm most grateful to those of you who have listened to my ponderings and have shared your own opinions. If and when I feel differently about writing and sharing, I hope you will allow me into your lives once again with my Thursday visits.

Warmly,
Beth

Printed in the USA
CPSIA information can be obtained
at www.ICGtesting.com
JSHW040928150224
57265JS00001B/1

* 9 7 8 1 9 1 6 8 5 2 5 0 1 *